THE FUNNIEST LIVERPOOL QUOTES... EVER!

About the author

Gordon Law is a freelance journalist and editor who has previously covered football for the *South London Press*, the *Premier League*, *Virgin Media* and a number of English national newspapers and magazines. He has also written several books on the beautiful game.

Also available to buy

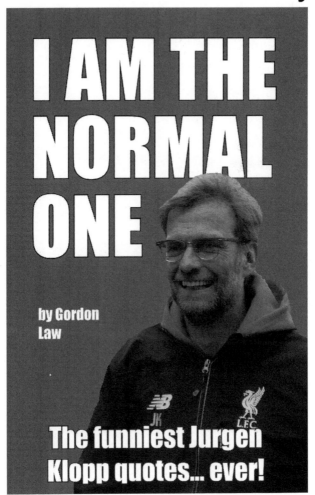

I AM THE NORMAL ONE

by Gordon Law

The funniest Jurgen Klopp quotes... ever!

Printed in the United States of America
ISBN-13: 978-1539859406
ISBN-10: 1539859401

Photos courtesy of: Maxisport/Shutterstock.com and Michael Hulf.

Contents

Introduction

"Some people believe football is a matter of life and death, I am very disappointed with that attitude. I can assure you it is much, much more important than that."

Liverpool manager Bill Shankly's iconic sound bite is arguably football's most famous ever, and it aptly describes the Scot's dedication to the club he led to unprecedented success.

While Shankly won plaudits for transforming the Reds from an average second division club into title-winning giants, it was his charismatic personality with a penchant for a comedic quip that made him an even more popular figure.

The Scot's endless supply of views on the game, his Liverpool players and the countless jibes at local rivals Everton are hilarious.

Bob Paisley not only continued Shankly's success as manager with an incredible 20 trophies in nine years, but he too had the knack of delivering a laugh-out-loud quote.

Fast forward a couple of decades and there's more head-scratching pronouncements and rants from the likes of Rafa Benitez, Brendan Rodgers and now, the eccentric Jurgen Klopp.

The sharp Scouse wit of Robbie Fowler, Steve McManaman and Jamie Carragher and the strange ramblings of Michael Owen have also been entertaining.

Many of their best one-liners and loads more can be found in this ludicrously funny collection of Liverpool quotations. Enjoy!

Gordon Law

THE FUNNIEST LIVERPOOL QUOTES... EVER!

PLAYER POWER

"I know Rafa [Benitez] well and he will break his own head to find a solution to get the title for Liverpool."

Pepe Reina on his manager's extreme measures

"Kenny Dalglish was quiet in the Liverpool team talks until the players started talking about conditions. Then he came on like a Govan shop steward."

Graeme Souness

"[Jose] Mourinho is the funniest thing to come out of London since Del Boy and Rodney."

Jamie Carragher

"Incey keeps you on your toes because he never stops moaning."

Jamie Redknapp on Paul Ince

"Friends ask me whether Rafa's cold attitude p*sses me off, but it doesn't. My aim is still to get a 'well done' off him before I retire. But then, if he gives me a 'well done' I might need a long lie down."

Steven Gerrard on Rafa Benitez

Q: "What would you have been if you hadn't been a footballer?"

A: "A virgin."

Peter Crouch

"We do things together. I'd walk into the toughest dockside pub in the world with this lot because you know that if things got tough, nobody would bottle it and scoot off."

Emlyn Hughes on his Liverpool teammates

"I'm no angel but I think I'm more misunderstood than anything else. I think I'm a pretty interesting bloke."

Stan Collymore in 1997

"I've seen myself referred to as 'a legend'. I've been called worse, let's put it that way."

Robbie Fowler

"I spoke to him just before he was getting on his flight and asked, 'Is it Kenny now or gaffer?' He said, 'It's Kenny now'."

Jamie Carragher the day after Kenny Dalglish was fired as manager in 2012

"I probably don't move as gracefully as people like Phil [Coutinho]. I'm a geezer in his mining boots from Yorkshire, lumping across the field!"

James Milner

"We didn't know what he was talking about half the time but we knew what he wanted."

Tommy Smith on Bob Paisley

Q: "Why don't Liverpool's young players ask you for advice?"

A: "Maybe it's because I don't speak English or something."

Luis Suarez

"The way Frank Worthington's losing his hair, he'll be the first bald guy to do impressions of Elvis Presley."

Graeme Souness

"When I ran towards The Kop I could almost hear them saying, 'Who's this skinny little tw*t?'"

Steven Gerrard on his debut in 1998, aged 18

"I didn't understand what the gaffer said. Then I typed both names into Google, so now I know."

Raheem Sterling after Brendan Rodgers said his skills were like 'Ricky Villa', but his finish was like 'Ricky Gervais'

"I've got more respect for [Alex] Ferguson than anyone else in the game. He's like a Scouser really. He's funny, doesn't mind telling people to f*ck off and he even votes Labour. I love him."

Jamie Carragher

"Come near me son and I'll break your back."

Tommy Smith to opposition players

"A boy from Croxteth should not use hair product."

Jamie Carragher on Wayne Rooney's 'new' hairstyle

"When I went to Liverpool, I must admit it was more of a culture shock than coming to France."

Joe Cole

"I dreamt of playing for a club like Manchester United, and now here I am at Liverpool."

Sander Westerveld

"If I was in Alex Ferguson's company, I would tell him first that Manchester United never knocked Liverpool off their f*cking perch, as he put it. That's nonsense. Graeme Souness did that."

Jamie Carragher believes former manager Souness was actually the architect of the club's downfall and not their bitter rivals

"One of my great regrets is that I got the chance to speak to Bill Shankly only the once. After I signed for Liverpool, John Toshack took me to Shanks' house to meet him. He gave me two pieces of advice: don't over-eat and don't lose your accent."

Kenny Dalglish

"I never saw Razor hit Robbie in the airport, just the trail of blood going through the green customs exit."

Stan Collymore on an altercation between Neil Ruddock and Robbie Fowler

"Sometimes I feel I'm hardly wanted in this Liverpool team. If I get two or three saves to make I've had a busy day."

Ray Clemence

"It's a huge honour to wear no.7 at Liverpool. I think about the legends: Dalglish, Keegan and that Australian guy."

Luis Suarez forgot about Harry Kewell

"In the penalty shoot-out, [Jerzy] Dudek looked like a starfish with jelly legs."

Bruce Grobbelaar after the 2005 Champions League final

"When you come from a council estate in Liverpool, how you come across is important. You don't want to be seen as a biff – some busy b*llocks like Gary Neville or someone who has sold his soul like [David] Beckham."

Robbie Fowler

"I'm the kind of player who trains well every day. Do I sound like the teacher's pet?"

Yes you do, Jamie Carragher

"I was to learn that praise from Bob Paisley was rather like a snowstorm in the Sahara."
Graeme Souness

"When the ball hit the net I felt like running over to him to give him a big kiss but then I decided against it!"
John Arne Riise on Steven Gerrard after he scored the FA Cup final winner in 2006

"Anyone who doesn't learn from Ian Rush needs shooting."
Robbie Fowler

"[Lionel] Messi can do some amazing things, but anything he can do Joe can do better."

Steven Gerrard on new signing Joe Cole

"They compare Steve McManaman to Steve Heighway and he's nothing like him, but I can see why – it's because he's a bit different."

Kevin Keegan

Q: "How would you define Dutch people in THREE words?"

A: "Dutch people generally are loyal, disciplined and straight to the point."

Ryan Babel in the Liverpool match-day programme

THE FUNNIEST LIVERPOOL QUOTES... EVER!

CALL THE MANAGER

"My players travel more than Phileas Fogg in 'Around The World In 80 Days'. Javier Mascherano had to play a friendly for Argentina in Australia. That must have been really important."

Rafa Benitez on his players featuring in international matches

"If one game should change my mind then I would be a real idiot."

Jurgen Klopp when asked if he was going to reconsider buying new players after losing to Burnley

"It was a perfect away performance, apart from the first 10 minutes."

Brendan Rodgers on a 2-0 defeat by Zenit St Petersburg – both goals came in the second half

"We were caviar in the first half, cabbage in the second."

Phil Thompson on Liverpool's display at Charlton

"Sadly, I have been unable to persuade FIFA, UEFA and the Premier League to allow me to use 12 players in every game."

Rafa Benitez on his rotation policy

"Because we weren't good enough, the linesman thought, 'You don't make world-class goals if you play this sh*t' so [you don't get the goal]."

Jurgen Klopp jokes the assistant referee didn't think his side deserved to score after he wrongly flagged Alberto Moreno offside against Newcastle

"The problem was conceding four goals in the first half."

Rafa Benitez was much happier with the second 45 minutes

"I'm not giving secrets like that to Milan. If I had my way I wouldn't even tell them the time of the kick-off."

Bill Shankly on being asked if he'd name a changed line-up to his side

"Luis has darker hair than me. I think Lawro must have been watching the radio."

Kenny Dalglish after Mark Lawrenson compared him to Luis Suarez

"The best word I can say to describe this is: Boom!"

Jurgen Klopp perfectly sums up the 3-0 triumph over Manchester City

"It was the most difficult thing in the world, when I went to tell the chairman. It was like walking to the electric chair. That's the way it felt."

Bill Shankly on leaving Liverpool

"It's like being given the Queen Elizabeth to steer in a force 10 gale."

Bob Paisley on replacing Bill Shankly

"I know I may come over as a miserable git, but that was kamikaze defending. Managers would be dead within six months if every game was like that."

Roy Evans after a 4-3 win over Newcastle

"Until now it's been OK. I'd really like to change my personality, but I can't forget this f*cking loss against Crystal Palace. If we had won this maybe then I would have said it was more than OK."

Jurgen Klopp is content with the start to his Liverpool tenure – except for a loss to Crystal Palace

"If you have a car and you win a race, you cannot just settle for that. You must try and make the car better. We're a good car but you always want a bigger engine"

Rafa Benitez

"I will not take some pills to stop me from celebrating a goal."

Jurgen Klopp when asked if he'd celebrate the Reds scoring against his former club Borussia Dortmund

"The second half was a crazy game and when it is a crazy game you can't control things. Why was it crazy? Because it was crazy."

Rafa Benitez on Liverpool's draw with Wigan Athletic

"What can you do, playing against eleven goalposts?"

Bill Shankly after a 0-0 draw at home

"He taught me a new phrase because he said he was 'over the moon' to be back at Liverpool and I had never heard that before."

Rafa Benitez learns some new lingo from Robbie Fowler

"There were two buses parked today, never mind one."

Brendan Rodgers after claiming Jose Mourinho's Chelsea played a six-man defence in their 2014 victory at Anfield

"I'm surprised they don't charge me rent and rates."

Bob Paisley after his 11th visit to Wembley

"Sickness would not have kept me away from this one. If I'd been dead, I would have had them bring the casket to the ground, prop it up in the stands and cut a hole in the lid."
Bill Shankly after Liverpool beat Everton in the 1971 FA Cup semi-final

"What do I say to them in the dressing room? Nothing really. Most of the time I don't even know what they are going to do myself."
Kenny Dalglish

"The pitch was terrible. The ball was like a rabbit and it's difficult to catch a rabbit."
Rafa Benitez

"This is the second time I've beaten the Germans here... the first time was in 1944. I drove into Rome on a tank when the city was liberated."

Ex-soldier Bob Paisley after Liverpool beat Borussia Monchengladbach to win the 1977 European Cup, in Rome

"I am enjoying this result and concentrating on coaching and training my players."

Rafa Benitez repeated this between nine and 25 times (depending on which paper you read) after he was told by the board not to criticise their transfer policy

"For me it's been a good season, but we've only made a cake. Now we need to put the cherry on top."

Rafa Benitez

"The best side drew."

Bill Shankly after a hard-fought 1-1 draw

"You may have found me mean and thirsty in my search for trophies, but the bad news is the man who is taking my place is hungrier than me. Fagan's the name and I don't think he'll need any help from the Artful Dodger!"

Bob Paisley on Joe Fagan

"I am not going to call myself anything. I am a normal guy from the Black Forest. My mother is watching this press conference at home. If you are going to call me anything, call me the Normal One. I was a very average player and became a trainer in Germany with a special club."

Jurgen Klopp after being asked by reporters if he was also a 'special one' during his first Reds press conference

"I wished him good luck. He's a good manager and his English is better than I thought!"

Gerard Houllier on Rafa Benitez

A FUNNY OLD GAME

"Some of the [football] jargon is frightening. They talk of 'getting round the back' and sound like burglars. They say, 'You must make more positive runs' or 'You're getting too negative' which sounds as if you're filling the team with electricians."

Bob Paisley, 1980

"Some fruit and vegetable dealers did very well."

John Barnes after Everton fans threw bananas at him

"[Frank] Sinatra would kill to sing here."

Bill Shankly on the Liverpool atmosphere

"I would kick my own brother if necessary. That's what being a professional footballer is all about."

Steve McMahon

"People who sit in the stands perhaps don't realise the extra pressure exerted by the emotional side of the game. It's not easy to cope with and it's quite possible to become drunk on four ounces of wine gum!"

Bob Paisley

"I love tackling. It's better than sex. A great tackle gets everybody pumped up."

Paul Ince

"The magic of the FA Cup was bloodied on the day my penis was cut and then stitched shut on an unromantic afternoon in Bournemouth last year. It was eye-watering. I tried to close down a winger to block his cross but felt a stinging in my privates. I thought, 'Sh*t – that doesn't feel right!' It was stinging like f*ck. The gash looked pretty bad, right across the middle. There was plenty of blood. I needed four stitches and the lads were absolutely p*ssing themselves."

Steven Gerrard in his book 'My Story'

"I hate talking about football. I just do it, you know?"

Robbie Fowler

"If I told people that the secret of Liverpool's success is a dip in the Mersey three times a week, I not only reckon they'd believe me but I think our river would be full of footballers from all over the country."

Ronnie Moran

"Football is a simple game made complicated by people who should know better."

Bill Shankly

"My eyes water when they sing 'You'll Never Walk Alone'. I've actually been crying while playing."

Kevin Keegan

"If he isn't named Footballer of the Year, football should be stopped and the men who picked any other player should be sent to the Kremlin."

Bill Shankly on Tommy Smith

"By the time referees are finally experienced enough to understand the teams and what players are trying to get away with, it's time for them to retire."

Rafa Benitez

"I don't enjoy games much. I'm not a skilful player who can have much fun on the pitch."

Javier Mascherano is miserable

"I'm not allowed to wear gloves. When I was about 12, my dad came to watch me play. I bought a pair of gloves out and he walked off!"
Steven Gerrard

"A football team is like a piano. You need eight men to carry it and three to play the damn thing."
Bill Shankly

"I was thinking I should kiss the penalty spot, the grass and the post. I think every Liverpool player should do that."
Jerzy Dudek after finding out he was picked to play in the 2005 Champions League final

"There are those who say maybe I should forget about football. Maybe I should forget about breathing. As Arnold Schwarzenegger said, I'll be back."

Gerard Houllier says he will return as boss after he recovers from cardiac surgery

"I swear that when we first walked out onto the pitch most people thought we were the band."

Robbie Fowler on the squad's white suits they wore for the 1996 FA Cup final

"The trouble with referees is that they know the rules but they don't know the game."

Bill Shankly

"My favourite letter [I received] is the one which said, 'You, Smith, Jones and Heighway had better keep looking over your shoulder. You are all going to get your dews'."

Emlyn Hughes

Bill Shankly: "Where are you from?"

Liverpool fan: "I'm a Liverpool fan from London."

Bill Shankly: "Well laddie... What's it like to be in heaven?"

"I was only a kid when Liverpool last won the league. In fact I was still an Everton fan."

Michael Owen

THE FUNNIEST LIVERPOOL QUOTES... EVER!

BEST OF ENEMIES

"We were good friends until we started winning, then he started changing his mind," **Rafa Benitez is no longer matey with Jose Mourinho**

"Brian Clough is worse than the rain in Manchester. At least God stops that occasionally."
Bill Shankly

"If anyone ever mentions the Everton 'School of Soccer Science' to me again, well, I'm sorry, I just don't see it."
Roy Evans

"What do you think they're smoking over there at the Emirates?"

John W Henry on Arsenal's £40,000,001 bid for Luis Suarez

"I wasn't disappointed with his comments because I know the man."

Gerard Houllier on Paul Ince who claimed the former manager and his no.2 Phil Thompson were "two-faced and treat people like dirt" on leaving in 1999

Reporter: "Where's [now retired] Bill Shankly?"

Bob Paisley: "He's trying to get right away from football. I believe he went to Everton."

"I was watching a TV programme about accents where they said the Birmingham dialect was the most difficult to understand, so I couldn't make out what they were saying."

Rafa Benitez on getting abuse from Aston Villa fans

"Sometimes if you spit up in the air, it can come back in your face."

Gerard Houllier responds to Crystal Palace striker Clinton Morrison's barbs

"Of course there are two great teams on Merseyside. Liverpool and Liverpool reserves."

Bill Shankly

"It's not hard to coach 10 players to be on the edge of the 18-yard box."

Brendan Rodgers makes a dig at Jose Mourinho after Chelsea won at Liverpool

"When you play against the smaller clubs at Anfield, you know the game will be narrow."

Rafa Benitez has a swipe at Everton after a frustrating draw

"Don't worry Alan. At least you'll be able to play close to a great team!"

Bill Shankly to Alan Ball who signed for Everton

"We don't need to give away flags for our fans to wave. Our supporters are always there with their hearts, and that is all we need. It's the passion of the fans that helps to win matches, not flags."

Rafa Benitez has a dig at Chelsea

"A mate owned a Bryan Robson top. We were kicking about, and I asked if I could be Robbo for a while. My dad looked out and went ballistic. He wasn't having his kid dragging the Gerrard name through the gutter. I thought we'd have to move!"

Steven Gerrard

"The difference between Everton and the Queen Mary is that Everton carry more passengers!"
Bill Shankly

"It was United's ground, mostly their fans, but it was our ball."
Brendan Rodgers on the 3-0 win over Man United in 2014

"I guess when you've invested £500milion it's a fantastic season to win the League Cup."
A sarcastic Reds chief executive Rick Parry on Chelsea

"I think Spurs ought to buy a good stock of cotton wool for such poseurs. He can't expect not to be tackled just because Argentina won the World Cup."
Tommy Smith on Ossie Ardiles

"Two finals in three years – not bad for a little club."
Steven Gerrard after the Reds beat Chelsea to reach the Champions League final in 2007. Jose Mourinho had labelled them "a little club"

"Liverpool are magic. Everton are tragic."
Emlyn Hughes

"To me, Arsenal play much better football. They win matches and are exciting to watch. Barcelona and Milan too. They create excitement so how can you say Chelsea are the best team in the world?"

Rafa Benitez after Chelsea held Liverpool to a 0-0 draw in a Champions League group game

"When I've got nothing better to do, I look down the league table to see how Everton are getting along."

Bill Shankly

"I think what he does is a model for other managers around the world – it's a perfect model for all the kids as well. As for the style of football, even Barcelona are now copying his style."

A sarcastic Rafa Benitez on Sam Allardyce

"If Everton were playing down the bottom of my garden, I'd draw the curtains."

Bill Shankly

"I would've been really sad and disappointed to see Luis [Suarez] go to Arsenal. With all due respect to them, I told him he was too good for Arsenal."

Steven Gerrard

"Mourinho talks a lot about a lot of people, but I prefer to talk about facts. At Liverpool, with a squad half of the value of Chelsea, we twice knocked his Chelsea side out of the Champions League. Later, with the most expensive squad at Real Madrid, he did nothing in the Champions League. Now he says if there is an offer of hundreds of millions for Hazard and Oscar, maybe he can build a strong squad to win something."

Rafa Benitez on Jose Mourinho's record

"Training changed as soon as [Gerard] Houllier arrived. There was no enjoyment allowed. It was f*cking miserable."

Robbie Fowler

"We have our special ones here, they are our fans, who always play with their hearts."

Rafa Benitez has a dig at the 'Special One' Jose Mourinho

"107 caps isn't bad for someone who isn't 'a top, top player,' is it?"

Steven Gerrard after Sir Alex Ferguson claimed he wasn't "a top, top player"

"We have got a lot more expensive failures on our list than good players that we have brought in for next to nothing."

Roy Hodgson takes a swipe at the signings made by predecessor Rafa Benitez

"Until now when I've met an Evertonian, nobody has knocked me, nobody kicked me. It's always nice. Nothing happened."

Jurgen Klopp

"I'm sure Chelsea do not like playing Liverpool. When they are talking and talking and talking before the game it means they are worried. Maybe they're afraid?"

Rafa Benitez on the 2007 Champions League semi-final tie

Barber: "Do you want anything off the top?"

Bill Shankley: "Aye, Everton."

Q: "Did you and Grobbelaar continue the fisticuffs in the changing room at Goodison? And did he use his shaky-leg tactic to psyche you out?"

A: "No, not really. It ended there and then. A couple of slaps and punches and there it ended. And yeah, his spaghetti legs absolutely terrified me..."

Steve McManaman on the pitch bust-up with Bruce Grobbelaar in 1993

"He says he's a Red, but they all say that when they sign, don't they?"

Steven Gerrard on new teammate Craig Bellamy's claim to be a lifelong Liverpool supporter

"I know this is a sad occasion but I think that Dixie would be amazed to know that even in death he could draw a bigger crowd than Everton can on a Saturday afternoon."
Bill Shankly at Dixie Dean's funeral

"With [Didier] Drogba it's important to have a good referee. You can't do anything [to stop him going down], but I will say it because it was so clear. He is amazing because he is massive [yet he goes down]. It's very impressive. I have a lot of clips of him from over the years and he surprises me. After four years I expected it. It's very impressive."
Rafa Benitez

"He's the England right back and, if he plays like that, one would expect him to come back in when he's fit. But then he'd have to play like the England right back and up to now, to be quite frank, he's not performed – very often at least – to the level I'd expect of him. You would have to ask him 'do you think you're playing like the best right back in the country for your club?' If he says yes, obviously we will have to agree to differ."

Roy Hodgson in a surprising public attack on Glen Johnson

"Leeds United are having problems with injuries. The players keep recovering."

Bill Shankly on Leeds' poor run of form

"If you've had three years at Chelsea and spent that kind of money and not got to the Champions League final, you might be in trouble from the owner!"

Jamie Carragher takes a swipe at Jose Mourinho after Liverpool beat Chelsea in the 2007 Champions League semi-final

"Chelsea is a big club with fantastic players and every manager wants to coach such a big team. But I would never take that job, in respect for my former team at Liverpool, no matter what. For me there's only one club in England, and that's Liverpool."

Rafa Benitez – before he ended up joining Chelsea as interim manager

[Pulling a piece of paper from his pocket] "But I want to talk about facts. I want to be clear, I do not want to play mind games too early, although they seem to want to start. But I have seen some facts... There is another option. That Mr Ferguson organises the fixtures in his office and sends it to us and everyone will know and cannot complain... We had a meeting in Manchester with managers and FA about the Respect campaign. And I was very clear, forget the campaign because Mr Ferguson was killing the referees. But he is not punished. How can you talk about the Respect campaign and criticise the referee every single week?"

Part of the Rafa Benitez 'fact' rant where he claimed Alex Ferguson had preferential treatment with the fixtures and referees

"You'd be better off talking to my baby. She's only six weeks old but you'd get more sense from her than him."
Kenny Dalglish on Sir Alex Ferguson

"If Chelsea are naive and pure then I'm Little Red Riding Hood."
Rafa Benitez after Jose Mourinho said his side were "naive, pure and clean"

"Give them these when they arrive – they'll need them!"
Bill Shankly hands a box of toilet rolls to the doorman for the Everton team for when they arrive at Anfield

THE FUNNIEST LIVERPOOL QUOTES... EVER!

TALKING BALLS

"I use a quote with the players, 'per aspera ad astra', which is Latin for 'through adversity to the stars."

Brendan Rodgers

"Too many players were trying to create or score a goal."

Gerard Houllier after a Liverpool defeat to Watford

"I couldn't settle in Italy – it was like living in a foreign country."

Ian Rush after returning from his spell with Juventus

"Liverpool is special. It is a special team, with special fans and a special city and I am happy to live in this city and to play for this special club."

Fernando Torres has special feelings

"I have a good record there. Played one, won one, and hopefully it will be the same after Saturday."

Steven Gerrard

"He's put on weight and I've lost it, and vice versa."

Ronnie Whelan

"Today's top players only want to play in London or for Manchester United. That's what happened when I tried to sign Alan Shearer and he went to Blackburn."

Graeme Souness

"Djimi Traore had to adapt to the English game and he did that by going out on loan to Lens last season."

Ian Rush confuses France with England

"We had a good plan in the first half but conceded two goals, so you can throw your plan in the purple bin."

Jurgen Klopp on his 'purple bin'

"Last year I had a foot operation. Then my thigh went. This season I'm going to play it by ear."

John Aldridge

"I'm a people's man, a player's man. You could call me a humanist."

Bill Shankly

"You can't say my team aren't winners. They've proved that by finishing fourth, third and second in the past three seasons."

Gerard Houllier

"Carra doesn't like me to fist him before the games, so I give him a high-five instead."
Pepe Reina on pre-match rituals with Jamie Carragher

"The champions are the team with the most points... if United have more points, it means they have more points, that's all. Nothing else"
Rafa Benitez after Man United beat Liverpool to the title in 2009

"I was there the night Jock Stein died, and I want to go when I'm in bed with my beautiful young wife."
Graeme Souness

"Sometimes you open your mouth and it punches you straight between the eyes."

Ian Rush

"Pat Crerand is deceptive: he's slower than you think."

Bill Shankly

"All derbies are the same, and this will be no exception."

Roy Evans

"Sir Alex is a work alcoholic."

Gerard Houllier

"You must wait until the end, and at the end of the season you can say it was a good or a bad season."

Rafa Benitez responds to talk of a crisis

"Have you seen my a*se? It's like an Alsatian's."

Steven Gerrard

"If they keep ramming it down his throat, the ball's in his court."

Roy Evans

"It was not a mistake, it was a blunder."

Gerard Houllier

"If Rafa said he wanted to buy Snoop Doggy, we would back him."

Co-owner George Gillett Jr on Rafa Benitez

"We know what we need to do now so I think we'll either win or lose."

Ian Rush

"I understand derbies. I love derbies. To be honest, it's the salt in the soup."

Jurgen Klopp on Liverpool vs Man United

"You train dogs. I like to educate players."

Brendan Rodgers to the press

"Like everyone else I get really immersed in the subject. I start looking through the eye of the microscope at the minuscule particles of dust, trying to see if there is an atom there. Maybe it is just a bit of dust."

Roy Hodgson on Liverpool's start to the season

"Aim for the sky and you'll reach the ceiling. Aim for the ceiling and you'll stay on the floor."

Bill Shankly

"Coming from Jamaica, I am blessed with rhythm."

John Barnes

"We have to talk with all LFC fans. Expectations can be a real big problem. It's like a backpack of 20 kilos. It's not so cool to run with this."

Jurgen Klopp on living up to the hopes of the Liverpool supporters

"We play with 11 men, other teams play with 10 men and a goalkeeper."

Brendan Rodgers

"One of the things I keep reminding players is that when you're lost in a fog, you must stick together. Then you don't get lost."

Bob Paisley

CAN YOU MANAGE?

"I think there's three players who will let us down this year – the cause, the fight, everything – and I have written them down already in these three envelopes. Make sure you are not in one of the envelopes."

Brendan Rodgers speaking to the squad in a TV documentary

"There are two sorts of fans – those that understand what we have been doing at this club and those who do not."

Gerard Houllier after finding offensive graffiti at the training ground in 2004

"I could play them all together. We could play 4-1-4! Hang on, I've forgotten a player haven't I? OK, 4-1-5!"

Jurgen Klopp briefly struggles with his maths when talking tactics against Crystal Palace

"They say we're predictable. Well Joe Louis was predictable. He'd knock his man down to the floor. Goodbye!"

Bill Shankly

"What I say to the players is this: 'The crown is on your head, my friend. You are the king of your destiny'."

Brendan Rodgers

"I've changed my routine since the heart surgery. I get in to work at 8.30am instead of 8am."

Gerard Houllier

"I know what's wrong – he's got a bad side!"

Bill Shankly on hearing a rival manager was unwell

"These young players are our future. If we handle them like horses then we get horses."
Jurgen Klopp

"I daren't play in a five-a-side at Liverpool, because if I collapsed, no one would give me the kiss of life."
Graeme Souness on losing his popularity

Richard Keys: "Well Roy, do you think that you'll have to finish above Manchester United to win the league?"
Roy Evans: "You have to finish above everyone to win the league, Richard."

"My scout told me this lad had football in his blood. I said, 'Aye, but it hasn't reached his legs yet'."

Bill Shankly

'My family are really happy here at Liverpool and I am prepared to have my daughter with a Scouse accent, even though it is sometimes a problem for me."

Rafa Benitez

"I enjoyed everything about the job – even the chants of 'Sit down Pinocchio'."

Phil Thompson

"I always enjoy the summer. You can't lose any matches."

Roy Evans

"I never wanted this bloody job, but it looks like you're stuck with me."

Bob Paisley's first talk with the players before his trophy-laden success

"I always say a squad is like a good meal – I'm not a great cook but a good meal takes a wee bit of time, but also to offer a good meal you need good ingredients."

Brendan Rodgers

"I've been described as a French revolutionary with a guillotine, but I prefer to convince people rather than dictate to them."

Gerard Houllier after steering Liverpool to a cup treble in 2001

"If you've got three Scots in your team you've got a chance of winning something. Any more and you've got trouble."

Bill Shankly

"I've always said that you can live without water for many days, but you can't live for a second without hope."

Brendan Rodgers

"I happen to like the aggravation that goes with football management. It seems to suit my needs."

Graeme Souness on becoming Liverpool manager in 1991

"I had problems at first, confusing 'wine' and 'win' and my players would laugh."

Rafa Benitez

"I was the best manager in Britain because I was never devious or cheated anyone. I'd break my wife's legs if I played against her, but I'd never cheat her."

Bill Shankly

"They'll be a formidable challenge – there's no question about that."

Roy Hodgson on facing mighty League Two opponents Northampton Town in the cup

"Liverpool without European football is like a banquet without wine."

Roy Evans

"I believe a young man will run through a barbed-wire fence for you. An older player looks for a hole in the fence."

Brendan Rodgers

"I recently met a famous brain surgeon in New York and in his brain, when it comes to intelligence, there are definitely 80 per cent more light bulbs alight than in mine. But what happens? He started to stutter because he is crazy about football and this person from LFC was suddenly standing in front of him."

Jurgen Klopp on being an idol

"I've been here during the bad times too. One year we came second."

Bob Paisley

"I don't drop players, I make changes."

Bill Shankly

"That was as good as we have played all season, and I have no qualms with the performance whatsoever. I only hope fair minded people will see it the same way."

Roy Hodgson on a derby loss to Everton

"To get a result here would have been Utopia. But I can only analyse the performance. There is no point trying to analyse dreams."

Another quote from Roy Hodgson after the Toffees defeat

"Winning trophies has made me put on weight."

Rafa Benitez

"The last 18 months we have been on a magic carpet ride of development but we still have a lot of growth to make."

Brendan Rodgers

"You have to get information in each situation. You'll never find me three days after a win, drunk in a hedge and still celebrating."

Jurgen Klopp when asked how Liverpool would recover from defeat to West Ham

"If you can't make decisions in life, you're a bloody menace. You'd be better becoming an MP!"

Bill Shankly

"I want to build a team that's invincible, so they'll have to send a team from Mars to beat us."

Bill Shankly

"I've always worked along with the statistic that if you can dominate the game with the ball you have a 79 per cent chance of winning the game."

Brendan Rodgers

"There is no solution. We do not have the tallest team in the league. How do you fix that? Make them taller!"

Jurgen Klopp

"He [Meireles] had two training sessions and played on Thursday night and he played again on Sunday so it is very early for me to make strong judgements about where his best position is. The work we do on the training field will show me how best to use him."

Roy Hodgson is not sure where he is going to play £10m midfielder Raul Meireles

"I said that when I took over that I would settle for a drop of Bell's once a month, a big bottle at the end of the season and a ride round the city in an open top bus!"

Bob Paisley

"When you've got the ball 65-70 per cent of the time, it's a football death for the other team. We're not at that stage yet, but that's what we will get to. It's death by football. You just suck the life out of them."

Brendan Rodgers... OK then?

"I knew he had a stomach problem because I was in the toilet after him."

Kenny Dalglish explains why he substituted Daniel Agger at half-time

"It is better to be here than, I don't know, North Korea or something. It feels good."

Jurgen Klopp

"When we lost at Stoke last season I got home on Boxing Day night and family and guests were all around the house. I went straight upstairs to my room and didn't come out."

Brendan Rodgers

"Me having no education. I had to use my brains."

Bill Shankly

"We had a lovely dinner with Kenny, his wife Marina and son Paul. I understood about half of what he said and just nodded when I couldn't understand."

Chairman Tom Werner on Kenny Dalglish's return as manager

WOMAN
TROUBLE

"Of course I didn't take my wife to see Rochdale as an anniversary present. It was her birthday. Would I have got married in the football season? Anyway, it was Rochdale reserves."

Bill Shankly

"After the game, Sheila [the Liverpool club secretary], who was sitting right in line, told me that ball had crossed the goal line. She's a very honest person and that was good enough for me."

Rafa Benitez on Luis Garcia's 'ghost goal' against Chelsea in the 2005 Champions League semi-final

"It's the equivalent to being with the prettiest woman in the world and only sleeping with her once a month. I prefer to sleep with someone slightly less pretty every night!"

Gerard Houllier doesn't fancy the England manager's job

"I can play anywhere on the park. I'm a bit like that in bed, too."

Steven Gerrard

"I've sold my wedding pictures to The Kop magazine for a pound."

Jamie Carragher after getting married in 2005

"Professional footballers should have more sense than to consider marrying during the season. Anybody who does isn't behaving professionally as far as I'm concerned."

Bill Shankly

"She thinks she's Jose Mourinho. Some of the stuff she's telling me, the manager is telling me as well. She really knows about the game."

Raheem Sterling on his mum's knowledge

"How can you tell your wife that you're just popping out to play a match and then not come back for five days?"

Rafa Benitez on watching Test cricket

Journalist: "Is it true you said you would tackle your own grandmother if necessary."

Bill Shankly: "Don't be stupid. She would have more sense than to come anywhere near me."

"I'll have my mobile on holiday with me and as long as my wife doesn't find it, I'll continue to work. If she does find it, maybe she will throw it into the swimming pool."

Rafa Benitez

"At first he told us to wear boxing gloves in bed on Friday nights, then later he would tell us to send the wife to her mother."

Ian St John on advice from Bill Shankly

"When I was at Valencia my wife said that we would win the league. She was right and to mark the occasion she asked me for a new watch. I bought her the watch, but then she said that we would win the UEFA Cup and that when we did she wanted another watch. Now she says that we will win the Champions League and that she will want an even more expensive watch. My wife has a lot of confidence and a lot of watches."

Rafa Benitez after his wife Montse predicted Liverpool would win the 2005 Champions League ahead of their semi-final tie with Chelsea

"I've been so wedded to Liverpool that I've taken [my wife] Nessie out only twice in 40 years. It's time she saw more of my old ugly mug."

Bill Shankly on retirement in 1974

"I got some girl's knickers through the post the other day but I didn't like them. To be honest, they didn't fit."

Jamie Redknapp

"Dennis Wise grabbed my tit. I had five finger marks around the nipple, like a love bite. That took some explaining to the missus."

Jason McAteer

MANAGING PLAYERS

"He couldn't play anyway. I only wanted him for the reserve team."

Bill Shankly after hearing Lou Macari had chosen Man United over Liverpool

"He reminds me of a hunting dog. When I want something specific done, he is very willing to learn."

Rafa Benitez on Jamie Carragher

"Without picking out anyone in particular, I thought Mark Wright was tremendous."

Graeme Souness

"Look laddie, if you're in the penalty area and aren't quite sure what to do with the ball, just stick it in the net and we'll discuss your options afterwards."

Bill Shankly to Ian St John

"I like having Xabi Alonso on the pitch because I can give him instructions so that the other managers can't understand."

Rafa Benitez on the advantage of working with fellow Spaniard Xabi Alonso

"Tommy Smith would start a riot in a graveyard."

Bill Shankly

"Our goalkeeping coach, Joe Corrigan, has done a fantastic job on David's mental side. Though you'll never get that part completely right, because all keepers are mental anyway."

Roy Evans on David James

"If you say you do not like [Peter] Crouch that means you do not know a lot about football."

Rafa Benitez

"The trouble with you, son, is that your brains are all in your head."

Bill Shankly to a Liverpool player

"Tommy Smith wasn't born. He was quarried."

Bill Shankly

"Kenny Dalglish calls his goals tap-ins until we come to the end of the season and we're talking money."

Bob Paisley

"Yes, he misses a few. But he gets in the right places to miss them."

Bill Shankly on Roger Hunt

"To Tommy Smith: Take that bandage off! And what do you mean your knee? It's Liverpool's knee!"

Bill Shankly to Tommy Smith

"Graeme tosses up before kick off with a gold plated credit card."

Bob Paisley on Graeme Souness

"With him in defence, we could play [comedian] Arthur Askey in goal."

Bill Shankly after signing defender Ron Yeats

"I talk to Carra… If you can understand him you can understand anyone."

Rafa Benitez on Jamie Carragher

"He's not that bad on the ball, but let's not beat about the bush and try to disguise the fact – he's had a bad start."

Roy Hodgson on Christian Poulsen

"You say Tony Hateley's good in the air. Aye, but so was Douglas Bader – and he had two wooden legs."

Bill Shankly to Tommy Docherty

"He dribbled through Spurs' defence like Ricky Villa, but his finish was more like Ricky Gervais."

Brendan Rodgers on Raheem Sterling

"Just go out and drop a few hand grenades all over the place son."

Bill Shankly to Kevin Keegan

"The White Pele? You're more like the White Nellie!"

Bill Shankly to winger Peter Thompson who couldn't replicate his fine form for England in the 1964 Brazil Jubilee Tournament for his club

"Glen Johnson has been fantastic in the left back position in the past three games. I don't recall anyone going past him except me. And that was during training."

Kenny Dalglish

Goalkeeper Tommy Lawrence: "Sorry boss I should have kept my legs closed."

Bill Shankly: "Don't worry son it's not your fault, it was your mother who should have kept her legs closed."

THE FUNNIEST LIVERPOOL QUOTES... EVER!

LIFESTYLE CHOICE

"I must admit I suffered a bit when I first came to England. But then I realised that there was nothing to be intimidated by, everybody had two legs."

Lucas Leiva on settling in his new country

"Sometimes I'd like to have a conversation with a friend in a restaurant without feeling I'm being watched. At this rate I will have to go on holiday to Greenland. But maybe the Eskimos would know me."

Fernando Torres struggles to adapt to life on Merseyside

"Barnsey's chucked me a couple of cast-offs, things he hasn't worn or he never really liked. A few years ago he gave me a jacket covered in the Chinese alphabet. I love it but it's a bit loud."

Barry Venison on John Barnes' choice of clothes

"In France if you say the players can have a drink, they have two. Here they have double figures."

Gerard Houllier

"He's like a mobile larder."

Xabi Alonso on Pepe Reina's love for food

"Of course a player can have sexual intercourse before a match and play a blinder. But if he did for six months he'd be a decrepit old man. It takes the strength from the body."
Bill Shankly, 1971

"I compare top players to racing cars. Drinking alcohol is as silly as putting diesel in a racing car."
Gerard Houllier

"I'd certainly like to be as big as Lara Croft one day."
Michael Owen launching his own computer game

"You drink tea at four o'clock in the afternoon and nobody else knows why in the rest of the world. You drive on the wrong side of the road. We are different."

Jurgen Klopp

[Shortly after winning the FA Cup in 1974]

Bill Shankly: "Can I have some fish suppers?"

Chip shop server: "Mr Shankly, shouldn't they be having steak suppers?"

Bill Shankly: "No lass, they'll get steak suppers when they win the double!"

"I always had my packet of chocolate buttons."

Peter Beardsley

"Scouse people are very respectful. If they see me walking my dogs in the park, they say, 'Alright Nando, lad'. And that is all. I like that."

Fernando Torres

"He's a walking advert for the benefits of junk food. He'll eat five packets of crisps and wash it down with Coke and Mars bars."

Mark Lawrenson on Steve Nicol

"Hopefully we'll play better than my understanding of Scouse! It is still pretty difficult for me, especially if somebody speaks as quickly as possible – then I'm completely out!"

Jurgen Klopp

Robbie Fowler: "I know someone who had a w*nk two hours before a game and went out and scored a hat-trick."

Steve McManaman: "I know him. He captains his country. But I think the no-sex thing is a load of sh*te really."

Magazine interview in 1995

"There used to be a drinking culture in football and I know because I was part of it."

John Aldridge

"It's not nice going to the supermarket and the woman at the till thinking, 'Dodgy keeper'."

David James

"I'm nicknamed Trigger after the character in Only Fools and Horses because I'm basically thick. It came about in my Liverpool days when a waitress asked if I wanted my pizza cut into four pieces or eight. I said four because there was no way I could eat eight."

Jason McAteer

"I understand television without subtitles, so that is a good thing."

Jurgen Klopp on moving to England

"I was even recognised on the great wall of China!"

Steve McManaman

"I realise now that computer games have affected my performance badly. The last time I had a nightmare was at Middlesbrough in the Coca-Cola Cup and I had played Nintendo for eight hours beforehand."

David James

"I love to run on the streets around here. I love seeing the people going about their business. These are our people. I love running late in the afternoon, when the doors are open and the dinners are on, and you can smell the mince cooking…"

Brendan Rodgers

MEDIA CIRCUS

"As soon as I arrived in England I didn't like the press. They have never judged me on how I play football; they judged my attitude. The media said I dived, moaned, postured, they said I was racist, everything. They have never spoken well of me."

Luis Suarez

"I look a little bit like a serial killer, but you [the reporter] have ones like that too so you are used to it."

Jurgen Klopp when asked by a journalist if he was sporting new glasses after losing his old pair days earlier at Norwich

"So many sofa experts in this game...
Absolutely no idea about football what so
ever!"

**Glen Johnson after Liverpool threw away a
3-0 lead to draw 3-3 with Crystal Palace**

Radio Merseyside: "Mr Shankly, why is it
that your team's unbeaten run has suddenly
ended?"
Bill Shankly: "Why don't you go and jump in
the lake?"

"We've all talked the same nonsense over the
years. Everything you tell the press is a lie."
Jamie Carragher

"What do you mean, 'Do your methods translate?' They've translated from Halmstad to Malmo to Orebro to Neuchatel Xamax to the Swiss national team. So I find the question insulting. To suggest that, because I've moved from one club to another, that the methods which have stood me in good stead for 35 years and made me one of the most respected coaches in Europe suddenly don't work, is very hard to believe."

Roy Hodgson snaps during a disappointing run of form

"All the people told me about the British press, so it's up to you to show me you are all liars."

Jurgen Klopp

"I did not conduct myself in a way befitting of a Liverpool manager during that interview and I'd like to apologise for that."

Kenny Dalglish after he said that a TV interviewer was "out of order" to suggest Luis Suarez failed to shake Patrice Evra's hand in 2012

"They did not show this game on TV? They show every f*cking game in Germany."

Jurgen Klopp complains about the lack of TV coverage of Liverpool's cup victory against Derby

"It's part and parcel of being a footballer these days. I think a few of the lads would have liked to have seen a couple of them [the paparazzi] eaten by the lions."

Joe Cole is fed up with photographers following him and his England teammates during a safari trip in South Africa

"Don't know whether I said the right things but I tried to! I have got to get used to it but I have said this before, what appears in cold print isn't necessarily what you actually say."

Joe Fagan on his first press conference as Liverpool manager

"My mother's probably sitting in front of the television right now, watching this press conference, and not understanding a word I'm saying. But I'm sure she's very proud."

Jurgen Klopp after being unveiled as new Liverpool manager

"Just tell them I completely disagree with everything they say!"

Bill Shankly to a translator when being surrounded by rowdy Italian reporters

"I never liked pundits before I became one."

Alan Hansen

Reporter: "Are you concerned about the poor service to your strikers?"

Roy Hodgson: [Giving a long stare] "Are you from Denmark?"

Reporter: "No, I'm from Norway."

Hodgson: [Walking out of press room] "They are two countries I never want to work in again."

Exchange after Liverpool's 2-0 defeat to Everton

"Newspapers remind me of Jaws. They'll consume anything you've got and be back for more the next day."

Bob Paisley on the press

"You don't understand? You should learn. There are some really good German explanations for some problems. But I don't know how to say it in English."

Jurgen Klopp tries to get his message across to the British media

"Hold on a minute, John Wayne hasn't arrived yet."

Bill Shankly ahead of awaiting reporters before the press conference to announce his retirement from football